Contents

At school   2

Our pets   3

Buying pets   4

Feeding pets   5

Somewhere to sleep   7

Working pets   8

Guard dogs   9

Guide dogs   10

Hunting for food   11

Asking people   12

Portraits   14

Queen Victoria's dog 17

Photographs   18

Uncle Mick's parrots 20

At the museum   21

The Graham Children by William Hogarth (1697–1764)

The children in Mrs Williams' class talked about their pets.

Gemma has a cat called Stan.
He is older than she is.
He is sixteen years old.

Louise has a guinea pig called Wednesday. Louise said, "She's called Wednesday because I bought her on a Wednesday."

Suraj said, "I have a dog called Rag. He likes to play ball with me."

Have you got a pet?
People have kept pets for a long time.
Let's look for clues.

Buying pets

Gemma's cat had come from a cats' home.
Louise got her guinea pig from a pet shop.

In the past pets were often sold in markets from stalls
like this. What kind of pet is this man selling?

Canary seller, Mickleton area

How do you think he took his stall home at
the end of the day?

Stan and Rag are fed with pet food from the supermarket.

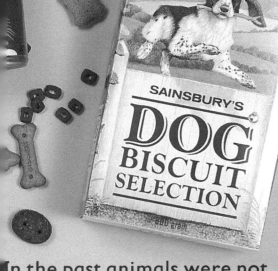

In the past animals were not given special food. They were given the scraps left from the table.

This is a picture of a very rich man five hundred years ago. He lets tiny dogs walk on the table. They were called 'table dogs'!

Do you let your animals walk on the table?

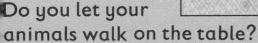

Book of Hours of the Duc de Berry, c. 1400

Enamelled advertisement, c.1910

This old advertisement shows a dog running away with dog biscuits.

Can you see the pet shop? Is it different from the supermarket?

Here is an old packet of bird seed. Someone bought it in a pet shop.

J and W Atlee, Dorking. (Cost: 4d) c.1910

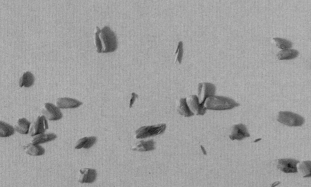

Somewhere to sleep

Where does your pet sleep?

This kennel was built for a dog called Dido. It was made to look like the house her owners lived in.

Ightham Mote, Kent, 1890

This picture is about five hundred years old. Do you let your pets sleep on the bed?

Tobias and Sarah, stained glass, c. 1530

Does your pet have to do any work?

Stan doesn't do anything. He likes to sleep all day. When he's not sleeping he likes to get in the way.

Sometimes people have pets to help them.

Rag works hard guarding the house. He barks every time a stranger walks up the path.

In the past people used dogs as guard dogs too.
This picture is from a Roman floor. It is made of tiny
coloured bits of stone. It is called a mosaic floor.
Someone made it about two thousand years ago.
It shows a Roman guard dog.

Mosaic, House of the Tragic Poet, Pompeii, first century AD

CAVE CANEM

It says 'Beware of the Dog' in Latin.

Guide dogs

This is a picture of a blind man. His dog helps him find the way.

Alfred Morgan with his guide dog Bella, 1936

This picture shows a blind man and his dog fifty years ago. Look at the cars and clothes.

Are they like the ones we have today?

Some animals help people hunt for food.

This man is holding two ferrets. Their long thin bodies help them run down holes and catch rabbits.

Mrs Williams' class wanted to find out more about pets in the past.

Mrs Williams said, "One way to find out is to ask some old people about the pets they used to have."

Louise's grandfather said, "I used to keep pigeons. Here's my photograph album.

Bishop Auckland Pigeon Club, 1954

Pigeons can fly back home from miles away. The men put their birds in baskets and sent them by train to another town.

Someone opened the baskets and the birds flew out. The first pigeon to get home was the winner."

Louise told the class all about this the next day.

Mrs Williams took her class to the school library and they looked for more pictures of pets in the past. Some of the pictures were paintings of people.

The Painter and his Pug by William Hogarth, 1745

"A picture of a person is called a portrait," said Mrs Williams.
"Rich people like to have portraits of themselves."

Sometimes people have their pets painted in their portraits.

William Hogarth was a portrait painter. He painted himself with his dog Trump.

Hogarth painted this portrait of the Strode family over two hundred years ago. The Strode's dog and Trump got into the picture too.

The Strode Family by William Hogarth, c. 1738

How can you tell this picture was painted a long time ago?

Here is a picture of Mr and Mrs Clark and their cat Percy. Do you think this was painted a long time ago?

Queen Victoria's dog

Hector, Nero, Dash and Lorey by Sir Edwin Landseer, 1837–8

Here is a picture of Queen Victoria's favourite dog Dash sitting on a stool.

Queen Victoria age 20, 1839

Victoria was only eighteen when she was crowned Queen. After the Coronation she went back to Buckingham Palace. The first thing she did was give Dash a bath.

Everyone wanted a picture of Dash so they sewed their own pictures to hang on the wall. The pattern was copied from the painting of Dash.

"Only a few people have their portrait painted now.
We have photographs taken instead," said Mrs Williams.

This photograph was taken eighty years ago.

These boys won a prize for their
guinea pigs. They don't look very happy.

Perhaps they had to wait a long time for
the photographer to take their picture.

Herbert and Arthur Jerman, c. 1906

This man kept pet canaries in his back room.

William Drake, canary breeder, c. 1900

Can you see some of his prizes on the table?

Couple with parrot, Weardale

These people look very proud of their parrot. Look at the cage.

A hundred years ago, one shop sold all these different shaped cages.

c. 1870

Steven said, "My Uncle Mick keeps parrots. They fly around but always come home again. I saw some baby parrots there once."

Mrs Williams took her class to the museum to look for more pets.

Gemma found an Egyptian cat.
It is helping its owner to catch birds.

Can you see the cat? It's hard to find.

Hunting wildfowl in the marshes, Egypt, c.1400 BC

Here it is!

This picture was painted about four thousand years ago. It shows that people have kept pets for a long time.

Suraj found a picture of a dog.
"Is it a wild dog or is it a pet one?" he asked.

Roman mosaic, Turkey, c. third century AD

Can you see the clue?
What can you see round its neck?
This is another picture from a mosaic floor.

Perhaps you could paint a picture
or take a photo of your pet for
people to look at in the future.

My Cat Pixie by Hannah Smithers, age 7